What?

Colleen L. Reece • illustrated by Lois Axeman • cover and title page designed by Mina Gow McLean • created by The Child's World

CP   CHILDRENS PRESS, CHICAGO

Library of Congress Cataloging in Publication Data

Reece, Colleen L.
  What.

  (Question books)
  Summary: Answers such questions as "What is love?
and "What causes toothaches?"
  1. Questions and answers—Juvenile literature.
[1. Questions and answers]   I. Axeman, Lois, ill.
II. Title.   III. Series.
AG195.R39   1983   031'.02   83-7308
ISBN 0-516-06591-2

What?

What is

Love is helping your
little sister tie her shoes.

Love is giving your
little brother a bite of
your candy bar.

Love is petting your
kitten or puppy.

love?

Love is feeling warm all over when Daddy hugs you. Or feeling close when Mother reads you a story.

Love is what you feel when your teacher smiles at you.

Love is something everyone needs.

What makes

When you stand in the sunlight, you make a shadow. This is because you are solid. Light cannot go through you! The light can go around you.

But the place where you keep the light from shining is dark. That place is your shadow.

If you move your arm or legs or head, your shadow changes. Try it and see!

my shadow?

You keep the sun from hitting what is behind
you when you move, too. So when you run, your
shadow follows you!

There are lots of things inside you! You need them all.

Inside you are bones. Without bones—especially your backbone—you would fall into a pile.

inside me?

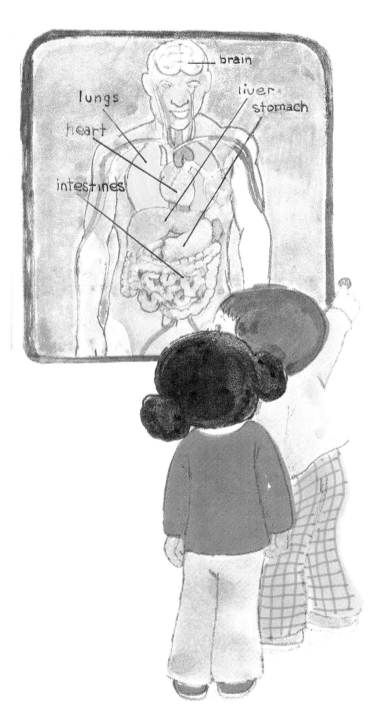

Two of the most important parts are your brain and heart.

Your brain acts like a computer. It stores things you learn.

Your heart works hard, sending blood through your whole body. It sends the blood through pipes, called veins.

(Most people have enough blood to fill a gallon milk carton with enough left to fill a quart juice bottle!)

You have many other parts. See some of them in the picture. When they all do what they should, you can run and play because you are strong and well. You are healthy!

What do animals

Some animals travel in winter. Birds fly south where it is warmer.

Deer come down to the valleys looking for food. So do wolves. Coyotes find warm holes to sleep in.

Hares and weasels in the north dress for winter! Their brown coats turn as white as snow. Then their enemies can't see them!

do in winter?

Squirrels and chip-munks are sleepyheads. They hibernate, or sleep, a long time. They only come out on sunny days.

But bears are the funniest of all! They stuff themselves so fat they can barely walk. Then they curl up in a den and sleep most of the winter!

What does a

A magnet pulls things of iron and steel toward itself. Magnets also stick to iron or steel. Magnets come in many shapes. Have you ever seen one in the shape of a horseshoe?

Magnets can be fun to play with. They can pull nails, pins, and other things to themselves.

People say a magnet "picks things up." Maybe it looks like that, but it doesn't. A magnet pulls things. And they come, just as a wagon comes when you pull on it.

magnet do?

There are giant magnets that work just as a horsehoe magnet does. They are used to lift and move heavy things.

Have you ever used a magnet to hold a note or a picture on the refrigerator? If not, ask Mom to give you a magnet. Then try it.

What are

Germs are tiny specks that live in or on plants and animals. They are so small they can only be seen through microscopes!

Some germs are called bacteria. Some bacteria are good. They help change milk into cheese and yogurt. Others live in our bodies. They help digest our food.

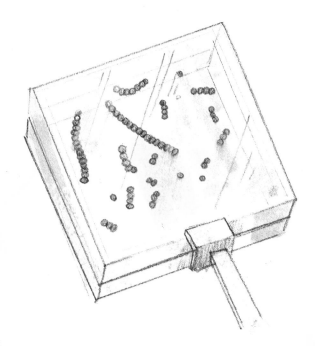

But some germs cause sickness. They make us feel awful. Some get inside cuts and scratches and cause an infection. These germs are bad for us.

germs?

Some bad germs can be killed by heat and soap. That's why we wash our dishes in hot soapy water. And that's why we wash our hands before we eat.

Other bad germs can be killed by medicine. If you get sick, the doctor may look in your throat and ears. He may give you some medicine. It helps kill the bad germs inside you. Then you will soon be well again.

What happens

When you laugh, small bursts of air come from your lungs. They travel up through your windpipe into your throat. The air makes your voice box move. HA! HA! HA! When something really tickles you, the air comes out of your mouth in funny sounds. A laugh!

Your face stretches and your mouth opens wide when you laugh hard. Sometimes your sides ache from all the small air bursts.

No two voices are just alike. Each sounds a little different. So does each laugh. That's why you can hear a friend laughing and know who he is even when you can't see him.

when I laugh?

If one of us laughs, others around us may laugh, too. Laughing makes everyone happy. So laugh!

17

What's beyond

Pretend you are standing on the smallest star in the sky. You are looking as hard as you can into outer space.

the stars?

You see stars and planets and moons. But you can't see them all.

Even the strongest telescope can't see all that's in space. Space is too big. Astronauts who have gone the farthest have seen just a tiny part of space.

Out past the stars is much more space. No matter how much we see, there will always be more.

19

What causes

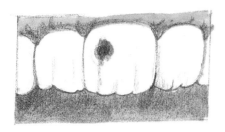

Did you ever get a hole in your coat? Could you feel the cold air come in?

Your teeth have coats, too! Sugar and food can tunnel right through those coats. They leave holes called "cavities." When you get holes in your teeth, you feel pain. This pain is a toothache.

You can do some things to fight cavities. Eat the right foods. Have regular checkups. Brush your teeth after you eat. And learn to use dental floss every night before you go to bed. This will stop food and sugar from making cavities. And *that* will keep you from getting toothaches!

toothaches?

What keeps

Moving air is wind. That's what keeps your kite up. You cannot fly a kite on a still day. You need the wind to push the kite into the air and keep it up.

As long as there is wind, the kite will stay up. But if the air stops moving, you'd better watch out for trees! Your kite will come down—fast!

my kite up?

What can

Perhaps you can take the dog for a walk. Or ask your dad if you can share an adventure. Maybe he will take you for a walk. You can make up names for all the cats and dogs you see along the way!

Have a friend help you plant seeds.

Ask your mom if you can make some popcorn. Then ask a friend to share it.

I do now?

Maybe you can make valentines. Or make Christmas or birthday cards.

You might even be able to:
Fingerpaint at the kitchen table. (Spread newspapers first!) Or make clay animals on the floor.

Just be sure to ask first!

We are tall or short, depending on the height of our parents and grandparents. If they are all tall, we probably will be tall. If they are all short, we probably will be short. This is not always true. But it usually is.

This is because we are born with tiny specks inside us called genes. These tiny specks decide what color our hair will be. They decide what color

us tall or short?

our eyes will be. And they decide how tall—or short—we will be.

Many children grow to be a tiny bit taller than their parents or grandparents. Perhaps this is because people eat better than they once did. And as we learn more about how vitamins and minerals help us grow, maybe we will grow taller yet.

What makes the

The sun and moon both work like magnets. They pull on the ocean waters. That makes the tide go in and out. The moon does most of the work, though. That's because the sun is so much farther away from the earth.

ide go in and out?

In most places, the tides "come in" and "go out" twice a day. And it's all because of the moon's hard work. Oh, yes—with a little help from the sun!

What happens

As you sleep, a lot of people are very busy!

Doctors and nurses take care of sick people.

Store workers put food on grocery shelves.

GROCERY STORE

HOSPITAL

Trains, trucks, and planes rush through the night. They carry mail and food and people!

when I'm asleep?

Factory workers and clean-up crews work at night.

Police officers, night guards, and firefighters stay up, too. They stay up to watch over things while you sleep.

People who work at night are just going to bed when you are getting up!